Greg Erhabor

The

seven

most effective

AFFIRMATIONS

towards achieving your

GOALS

**The Seven Most Effective Affirmations
Towards Achieving Your Goals**

Unless otherwise stated, all scriptures are taken from
the **New King James Version**

Published by Spokesman Communication Ministries,
P.O. Box 1154, Ile-Ife, Nigeria.

Printed in Nigeria

DEDICATION

To all who aspire to excel in all that pertains
to life and godliness, I dedicate this book.

CONTENTS

PREFACE TO
THE NEW EDITION

This book was last published three years ago and the first edition has been sold out. What naturally comes to mind is, why a second edition? Are there things I have experienced since it was first published? Are there things I need to rewrite or expunge from the book? How have I grown since the book was written?

Certain things come clearly to mind. I have become convinced beyond reasonable doubt that the words we speak will determine our destiny. Our lives try to catch up with our words. In a sense, our lives are self-fulfilling prophecies. For years, many mystical organizations have stressed the need to make affirmations and emphasize the power of mind over matter. However, I have come to realize that affirmations without true relationship with God could be detrimental because it makes man 'God.' Affirmations should flow out of our relationship with God. He is the invisible support that keeps the structure of life going. In presenting this edition, we must recognize that our source is from a definite relationship with God. Prayer is not just talking to God but communing with God.

Affirmation is the release of our faith; saying amen to our prayers and positively declaring what we have prayed for until it is answered. It is saying to God, 'Yes I believe.' As the Apostle Paul puts it, **"For with the heart one believes unto righteousness, and with the mouth confession is made unto salvation" (Romans 10:10).**

Our confessions establish our beliefs and pave way for our success in life.

INTRODUCTION

AFFIRMATION is a declaration. It is stating formally or confidently that something is true or correct. It expresses our agreement with a thing and indicates the word 'Yes.' This was the way Jesus lived His life. He said, 'I am the door.' 'I am the shepherd.' 'I am the light.' When you affirm, you are confessing a word with confidence. You are saying what you are.

Right from my youthful days, I have always been thrilled by the power of affirmation. The Bible declared, **"The tongue has the power of life and death and those who love it will eat its fruit" (Proverbs 18:21).** Paul told the Roman church, **"For it is with your heart that you believe and are justified and it is with your mouth that you confess and are saved" (Romans 10:10).**

This book on affirmations came about as a result of

something that has been burning in my spirit. However, I heard some of them from Robert Schuller, the Senior Pastor of Crystal Cathedral, Garden Grove in California. To him, I credit some of these affirmations. As a great philosopher said, "Next to the originator of a good sentence is the first quoter of it. Many will read the book before one thinks of quoting a passage. As soon as he has done this, that line will be quoted east and west. Then there are great ways of borrowing. Genius borrows nobly."

In this book, I am going to introduce seven affirmations, which if effectively used, will turn your dreams to reality and get your goals accomplished. We will also look at things you must not allow to happen to you when you set your goals.

Rev. Prof. Greg Erhabor

AFFIRMATION - ONE

I AM

"Jesus answered, 'I AM the way and the truth and the life. No one comes to the Father except through me" (John 14:6 NIV).

I AM is an affirmation of existence. It is a declaration of your personhood, of your own uniqueness and of your individuality. It is an assertion of who you are. It is saying, 'this is me' as contrasted to others. Do you know we are different? David wrote,

> **"For you formed my inward parts; you covered me in my mother's womb. I will praise you, for I am fearfully and wonderfully made, marvelous are your works and that my soul knows very well"** **(Psalm 139:13-14).**

'I am' is to come to terms with yourself. Many people will rather wish they were someone else. It is the power of saying 'I accept my uniqueness.' I acknowledge I am distinct.' Why spend your whole life thinking about someone else when you have enough inside you to make you the envy of others. Imitation, it has been said, is suicide. God in declaring himself the 'I am that I am' was affirming Himself. He is your Father and you can follow in His steps.

Goals and purpose have to do with who you are. They are not just activities; they are the expression of yourself. When you have a goal, you are saying, 'I am going to be this because God has made me who I am.' 'I am' is the initiating point of your goal.

For you to write your 'I am' or the goals that express your being, you must consult God. 'What have you prepared for me?' 'What is your plan for me?' As it were, you are saying to the Lord, 'Let me know your plan for me.' Paul said,

> **"For who has known the mind of the Lord that he may instruct Him? But we have the mind of Christ" (1 Corinthians 2:16).**

He told the Corinthian church,

> **"Now we have received, not the spirit of the world, but the spirit who is from God, that we might know the things that have been freely given to us by God" (1 Corinthians 2:12).**

The Hebrew writer said,

> **"Thus, God determining to show more abundantly to the heirs of promise the immutability of His counsel, confirmed it by an oath" (Hebrews 6:17).**

God's counsel is immutable. Therefore, the first point of achieving a goal is to say, 'I am a person created by God, for a purpose. I want to find it out.' 'This year God has a work for me to do. It is my duty to find it out and live it out on a daily basis.' When you come to the point of 'I am', goals become something that is born out of you. It is not another person's; it comes from you. Apart from coming from your spirit, it now burns in your bones. You know what God has written in His book concerning you; it burns in your soul. It gives you a burden like a woman who is pregnant.

You just catch it! It is not from without. Some people are others-driven while others are inwardly driven. Your drive now comes from within. When you know the 'I am', God becomes your boss. You can boldly say, 'God has a plan for me and I know it.' That has been the power behind great men of God. Robert Schuller, one of the great Christian ministers said he was invited as a young minister to speak in Norman Vincent Peale's church, which was one of the most beautiful churches in the world. He said, while he was in the vestry, a voice spoke to him. It said, 'Robert you have been called to build one of the biggest churches in the world, all made of glass.' At that instant, something rose up in him. Today, the Crystal Cathedral at Garden Grove, California has been built. It has become a reality.

I believe the same thing happened to Simon when Jesus said,

> "... You are Simon, the son of Jonah. You shall be called Cephas which is translated, a stone" (John 1:42).

It also happened to Jeremiah. The Lord told him,

> "Before I formed you in the womb I knew you; before you were born I sanctified you; I ordained you a prophet to the nations" (Jeremiah 1:5).

Right from his mother's womb, something burned in his spirit. He discovered his identity. The founder of "Bata" shoe felt he was called by God to "shoe" the world, and he saw his dream and vision turned to reality in his life time.

When you come to the point of defining your 'I am', something in your spirit burns. You will not accept any alternative. It is the push that propels one forward. Before you identify yourself, you might have said, 'Nobody is supporting me. I am alone.' But when you come to the 'I am', you now see a divine presence; a power flows into you.

I heard a minister preached sometimes ago. As he was preaching, I literarily saw his shoulders expanding and the Lord told me, 'That is the anointing.' The anointing arms you with strength. When you discover who you are in God, you do not have to worry about who follows you or who does not, because the mighty one is inside you.

Someone once commented: "There are two reasons why some people can not mind their own business. One is that they haven't any mind and the other is that they haven't any business." How can I see the dirt in your eye when I have much business to do? How can you know what another person is doing, when you have a job to do? Discovering who you are opens your eyes to your business and gives you the impetus to face it with zeal.

EPILOGUE - I AM

Do you know you are unique? God is not in the business of making duplicates. Are you thankful to God for who you are? Are you tempted to be jealous? Do you have a good estimation of yourself? List some of the qualities you consider your unique potentials; things that make you different.

....

....

....

....

....

....

....

....

....

....

....

Now, start to celebrate yourself. Develop and deploy your unique personality. You are God's number one!

Think about what you are on this earth to do. What is your purpose; your goal in life? How best can you describe yourself? Jesus said He is the Lamb of the world. John the Baptist called himself a 'voice.' Until you know your 'I am', you are just existing; you have not started living.

Write down who you are; your vision for existence. Think through it, fine-tune it and make it your focus. Don't give room to despair. Pray that God will help you to become who He wants you to be in Him.

AFFIRMATION - TWO

I CAN

"I CAN do all things
through Christ who
strengthens me"
(Philippians 4:13 NKJV).

I **CAN** is the affirmation of ability. If anybody is going to succeed in any goal-setting, he must go through the 'I CAN' phase. The Bible is filled with 'I CAN.' Paul wrote the Philippians:

"**But I rejoice in the Lord greatly that now at last your care for me has flourished again: though you surely did care, but you lacked opportunity. Not that I speak in regard to need, for I have learned in whatever state I am to be content: I know how to be abased and I know how to abound. Everywhere and in all things, I have learned both to be full and to be hungry, both to abound and to suffer need. 'I can do all things**

through Christ who strengthens me'
(Philippians 4:10-13).

This was a man who was confronted with many things that would have made men to give up. He faced impossible situations but rather than giving in to frustration, he boldly declared, "I can do all things through Christ."

Do you have exams? Declare with confidence: 'I can.' It is an affirmation of your ability. God is so particular about your 'I can.' Paul said,

> "But without faith it is impossible to please him, for he who comes to God must believe that He is, and that He is a rewarder of those who diligently seek Him" (Hebrew 11:6).

You must believe that you are capable because God is with you. Jesus said,

> "...For without me you can do nothing" (John 15:5).

And so with Christ, we can do all things. The spies

who were sent to the land of Canaan came back with critical analysis:

> "The people who dwell in the land are strong, the cities are fortified; we saw the descendants of Anak who were giants there" (Numbers 13:28).

The Bible said Caleb quietened them and said,

> "Let us go up at once and take possession, for we are well able to overcome it" (Numbers 13:33).

Caleb was simply saying 'we can.' Joshua also said, 'We can do it, with God being the umpire.' But the other spies opposed them. And God said,

> "Except for Caleb the son of Jephunneh and Joshua the son of Nun, you shall by no means enter the land which I swore I would make you dwell in" (Numbers 14:30).

Negative minded people never rise up to be great leaders. They will quench the enthusiasm and weaken the resolve of those they lead. Leaders are creative. They do not see impediments, they rather create opportunities. A leader rubs his spirit and attitude on his followers. This was what God was teaching us in the Scripture above. Leaders must always say 'we can.' David said to Saul, after he had tried to convince him against going to fight Goliath,

> **"The Lord, who delivered me from the paw of the lion and from the paw of the bear, he will deliver me from the hand of this Philistine" (1 Samuel 17:37).**

I can! And God gave him victory. **Ephesians 3:16** says,

> **"That he would grant you, according to the riches of His glory, to be strengthened with might through His spirit in the inner man."**

God has given us His ability. The greater one dwells in us.

> **"Now unto him who is able to do exceedingly abundantly above all that we ask or think**

according to the power that works in us'
(Ephesians 3:20)

Peter wrote in **2nd Peter 1:3,**

> **"His divine power has given to us all things that pertain to life and godliness through the knowledge of him who called us to glory and virtue."**

His power in us gives us strength and ability to do all things. Orison Swett Marden wrote, 'He can, who thinks He can, and he can't who thinks he can't. This is an inexorable and indisputable law.'

When you declare I can, you set in motion an immense power that has lied dormant in you. Your body also begins to respond and agree with your heart and you see yourself accomplishing your dreams and doing the impossible. It is not synonymous with pride or self conceit. Paul said, 'I can...through Christ.'

When you commit, God is compelled to act on your behalf. 'I can' is the voice that defeats fear, that puts timidity on the run and stirs the heavens to act on your behalf.

Whenever you declare 'I cannot', then you are sending the wrong signals to your body and it will follow it accordingly. That is the language the devil wants you to speak so he can have something to act upon. Quit saying 'I can't' and start declaring 'I can...through God.' Like Barrack Obama, the first black American President, declare 'Yes, I can.'

EPILOGUE - I CAN

Do you doubt your ability? Jesus said nothing is impossible to him that believes. Are you an 'I can' or an 'I can't' person? Giving excuses is a learned act, a habit that sticks to a man subtly. It becomes a philosophy that adheres to us. Pessimism is a disease of the mind. Liberate yourself now from the 'I can't' mentality. Think of all the challenges, assignments, duties and work that you must do. Write them down and state boldly: 'I can do these.'

....

....

....

....

....

....

....

....

....

....

....

....

....

Someone says, 'Impossibility lies in the dictionary of fools.' You are not a fool. The greater one dwells in you. He has given you His ability. Say loud before any task 'I CAN.' Yes, you can, through Christ that strengthens you.

AFFIRMATION - THREE

I MUST

"I MUST work the works of Him who sent me while it is day; the night is coming when no one can work" (John 9:4 NKJV).

I **MUST** is an affirmation of attitude. If you are going to succeed, you must come to the point where your attitude is that of magnificent obsession. Obsession means 'for a man to have a strong desire beyond rational thinking.' It cannot be rationalized. You cannot explain it. It is magnificent because the person is obsessed with a good thing.

If you want your goal to be accomplished, you must have this attitude of 'I must.' Jesus started the 'I must' theory when He said,

> **"I must work the works of Him who sent me while it is day; the night is coming when no one can work" (John 9:4).**

I must! The Bible said,

> **"From that time Jesus began to show to His disciples that he must go to Jerusalem and suffer many things from elders and chief priests and scribes, and be killed and be raised the third day"** **(Matthew 16:21).**

When you say **'I must'**, you do not apologize for the path that God has given you to tread. You would not say, 'God, I wish I had a better father,' 'I wish I never came to this town,' 'I wish I had a better husband or a better wife.' When men are prepared for greatness, their paths are usually rugged. No great man ever takes the crown who has never had the cross. Great men do not quarrel about the bridge they are about to cross. They say, 'I must cross the bridge.' They are not quitters. Jesus told His mother, **"Why did you seek me? Did you not know that I must be about my father's business?" (Luke 2:49).** If you want to be great, ask for the pathway of the Lord and follow it. As long as you have come to an **'I am'** and you have passed through **'I can'**, then you need to have the attitude of **'I must.'**

Paul knew that his calling was imperative. He wrote in **1 Corinthians 9:16,**

> "For if I preach the gospel, I have nothing to boast of, for necessity is laid upon me; yes, woe is me if I do not preach the gospel!" (NKJV)

When he was told about the challenges and difficulties he will face when he gets to Jerusalem, he replied,

> "Except that the Holy Spirit testifies in every city, saying that chains and tribulations await me, but none of these things move me nor do I count my life dear to myself so that I may finish my race with joy and the ministry which I received from the Lord Jesus, to testify to the gospel of the grace of God" (Acts 20:23-24).

When prophecies came to him that he would die in Jerusalem, Paul clearly declared that he was ready to be bound and even to die for the course of the gospel.

"And as we stayed many days, a certain prophet named Agabus came down from Judea. When he had come to us, he took Paul's belt, bound his own hands and feet and said, 'Thus says the Holy Spirit, so shall the Jews at Jerusalem bind the man who owns this belt and deliver him into the hands of the Gentiles. Now when we heard these things, both we and those from that place pleaded with him not to go up to Jerusalem. Then Paul answered, what do you mean by weeping and breaking my heart? For I am ready not only to be bound but also to die at Jerusalem for the name of the Lord Jesus" (Acts 21:10-13).

Think of a woman like Esther in the face of great challenges with threat to her life. She knew that the destiny of her people lies in her action yet she never hesitated when it was time to take a bold step. She said in **Esther 4:16,**

> **"Go gather together all the Jews that are present in Shushan and fast ye for me and neither eat nor drink three days, night or day: I also and my maidens will fast likewise; and so will I go in**

unto the king which is not according to the law:
and if I perish, I perish" (KJV).

Look at the 'I must' of Ruth, who remained faithful to
her mother in- law. In spite of the crisis, she held on to
the covenant of her youth. In **Ruth 1:16, 17** she said,

> "Entreat me not to leave you or to turn from
> following after you: for wherever you go, I will
> go: and where you lodge, I will lodge: your
> people shall be my people, and your God my
> God: where you die, will I die and there will I be
> buried: the Lord do so to me, and more also, if
> anything but death parts you and me."

These women had the **'I must'** attitude and became
great and notable for all generations to emulate.

Great men do not give excuses; they do the job at
hand. Don't excuse yourself out of your goal, vision
or purpose. George Washington Carver, a renowned
black American said, "Ninety-nine percent of failures
come from people who have the habit of making
excuses." Benjamin Franklin, a great American

statesman said, "He who is good at making excuses is seldom good for anything else." One writer wrote, "If half the ingenuity spent in finding excuses for not doing what we ought to do is put into what ought to be done, there would be a great difference." Find a reason why you must do your work. Somebody said, "We are all manufacturers; making goods, making troubles or making excuses. Decide what you want to manufacture."

Those who declare 'I must' have a single focus, distraction is not in their vocabulary. It is not to everything and to everyone that you must declare I must, you need to identify what is that role you must perform; that goal that you must achieve. What is that race that has been set before you? When you have identified this, then to that purpose you must say 'I must.'

Declaring 'I must' makes you to prioritize, to set first things first and then to commit yourself unreservedly to your number one goal. Without an 'I must' you become an 'everything goes' person. If you stand for nothing then you will fall for everything. Moreover, there should be no exit route to your purpose. What God has given you to do must be achieved. You must strive to meet up. Close all the escape routes. Don't look for an easy path. It is like a circle; you will come back to where you started from. Throw yourself into it and say to yourself, *'I must do the work.'*

EPILOGUE - I MUST

Are you used to giving excuses, or reasons for not doing your work? Do you weary your boss by your attitude to work? List the things you must do daily, weekly or yearly. List the common excuses you normally give in one column and then write out reasons in another column why you must do them. Make this a daily habit.

Things to do

....

....

Excuses for not doing them

....

....

Reasons I must do them

....

....

Pray that God will instill in you the **'I must'** attitude and help you to overcome the habit of giving excuses.

AFFIRMATION - FOUR

I WILL

"If you are WILLING and
obedient, you shall eat
the good of the land"
(Isaiah 1:19 NKJV).

I WILL is an affirmation of action. One man wrote a book titled, **'Success can be yours'** and the first chapter of that book was 'The will is king'.

> **"If you are willing and obedient, you shall eat the good of the land" (Isaiah 1:19).**

David said,

> **"I delight to do your will O my God…" (Psalm 40:8).**

It may be very difficult but he does not care! He went further in **Psalm 143:10** to say,

"Teach me to do your will for you are my God…"

Jesus said,

> **"Father if it is your will, take this cup away from me; nevertheless not my will but yours be done" (Luke 22:42).**

He asked the two blind men,

> **"What do you want me to do for you?" (Matthew 20:32)**

That is the language of the Scriptures. We were not told about the resolution of the apostles, we were only told about the Acts of the Apostles. When men say 'I will', they don't give any reason. They do not give any excuse. All they have to do is to obey the last command. Team strength is weakened by unwilling team mates. To achieve a purpose, all must resolve to get what they have set out to do. This is what I call the **'I will'** mentality.

'I will' is your resolute power to believe; to say to yourself that 'I must do what I must do.' Gothe, one of the great men of old, wrote, 'He who has a form will mould the world to himself.' Victor Hugo wrote, 'People do not lack strength, they lack will.' Paul encouraged the Church in Corinth on the need to first have a willing mind **(2 Corinthians 8:3).**

As Christians, our greatest quest should be to know God's will and do it. Jesus told us,

> **"My food is to do the will of Him that sent me, and to finish His work" (John 4:34).**

He said,

> **"For I have come down from heaven, not to do my own will but the will of Him who sent me" (John 6:38).**

Paul encouraged the Ephesians church,

> **"Therefore do not be unwise, but understand what the will of the Lord is" (Ephesians 5:17).**

He told the Roman church,

> **"And do not be conformed to this world but be ye**

transformed by the renewing of your mind, that
you may prove what is good, and acceptable, and
perfect will of God" (Romans 12:2).

However, once you are sure this is God's will, you
must affirm, 'I will.' Like Christ you must say: 'I
delight to do thy will O God.'

"Then said I, lo, behold, I have come in the
volume of the book, it is written of me, to do your
will, O God" (Hebrews 10:7).

We must be perfect in every good work to do His will.
No one can push you beyond your will. One great
American philosopher, said, 'The education of the
will is the object of our existence. For the resolute
and determined, there is time and opportunity.'

Louis Pasteur wrote, 'These three things: work, will,
success, fill human existence. Will opens the door to
success, both brilliant and happy, work passes the
doors and at the end of the journey success comes in
to crown one's effort.' Confucius made a great
statement, 'The general of a large army can be

defeated but you cannot defeat the determined mind of a peasant.'

W. Elderton wrote: 'Faint hearts, fair ladies, never win.' 'I will' is an expression of your heart; it shows you are interested in what you have to do, it shows you are enthusiastic about it. Your whole being is excited with it. It radiates in your face. Your willingness becomes contagious, with others around you catching it. Enthusiasm comes from the two words 'en' and 'theos' which means 'in' and 'God.' It is a demonstration of a life of divinity; of the fact that God is in us; expressing Himself through us.

Someone commented that the man who feels no enthusiasm for his work will never accomplish anything worthwhile. Emerson wrote, 'Every great and commanding moment in the annals of the world is the triumph of some enthusiasm.' It is better to have an enthusiastic novice to do a job than to have an unwilling genius. Greatness comes when we lighten our duties with fire and do our ordinary tasks with enthusiasm. Enthusiastic people rule the world.

EPILOGUE - I WILL

Do you have the will necessary to turn your thoughts into action? Have you sat down to really find out God's will for your life? Are you arranging your will according to environmental circumstances and people's opinions? List those things that you want to know God's will about. Once you know His will, exercise your will on them by putting them into action.

....
....
....
....
....
....
....
....

....

....

....

....

Pray that God will open your eyes to His will
and put in you the willingness required to
accomplish your purpose.

AFFIRMATION - FIVE

I AM INSTRUCTED

"I will INSTRUCT you and teach you in the way you should go: I will guide you with my eyes" (Psalm 32:8 NKJV).

If you are going to achieve your goal in life, you must be continually open to instructions. You must maintain a learning posture. All the opinions should not come from you. I have learnt to learn from everybody; from the youngest to the oldest.

In attaining your goal, you will need to be instructed. You will need mentors to pilot you as you face the challenges of life. Much more than that, you will need the Holy Spirit as a constant companion and help. This blessed impulse within you will give you unique wisdom and insight into the affairs of life.

Paul said, **"...I am instructed" (Philippians 4:12 KJV)** and I asked, 'Who has instructed him?' Isaiah gives us the answer,

> **"Your ears shall hear a word behind you, saying, 'This is the way, walk in it, whenever you turn to the right hand or whenever you turn to the left" (Isaiah 30:31).**

The instruction is continuous. Isaiah was saying that you will hear a voice instructing you, 'Turn to the right or turn to the left.' You must consistently and continually be prone to hear and to change. Life is a state of dynamism. Your character must consistently go through reformation. The word 'Born again' is in continuous tense. The Bible says we are gradually being metamorphosed. Do not become too rigid. Learn to respond to the message of Christ and grow.

Instruction is not just hearing, God will tell you what to do. Jesus said,

> **"But the comforter which is the Holy Ghost, whom the father will send in my name, he shall**

teach you all things and bring all things to your remembrance, whatsoever I have said unto you" (John 14:26 KJV).

He went further in **John 16:13** to say:

> "However, when He, the spirit of truth has come, He will guide you into all truth; for he will not speak on his own authority, but whatever He hears He will speak; and He will tell you things to come."

Isaiah said,

> "The Lord has given me the tongue of the learned, that I should know how to speak a word in season to him who is weary, he awakens me morning by morning, he awakens my ear to hear as the learned" (Isaiah 50:4).

Sometimes we make decisions in life that make us look like fools. I have always told God, 'Whenever I am behaving like a fool, please caution me.' Pray that God will help you to hear as the learned, so that when people see you, they will say, 'This man is in tune with

God.' Every staff recruited in any reputable establishment will need to undergo a training period when he will be instructed on the ethical standards.

The children of Israel, before any of their great wars, sought the mind of God through the prophet. Thanks be to God that today we have the Holy Spirit who can instruct us and show us the way. Jesus told his disciples that when they face the world's jury, they should not fear, for the spirit of the Father will teach them.

> **"Now when they bring you to the synagogues and magistrates and authorities, do not worry about how or what you should answer or what you should say. For the Holy Spirit will teach you in that very hour what you ought to say" (Luke 12:11, 12).**

He told them of the great events that will happen in the last days and what they will do when faced with opposition. This was demonstrated in the life of

Stephen, when facing his persecutors. He demonstrated such profound wisdom that they were astonished.

> **"And they were not able to resist the wisdom and the spirit by which he spoke" (Acts 6:10).**

Daniel demonstrated this wisdom when he and his companions were told to unravel the riddle of King Nebuchadnezzar's dream. We were told in **Daniel 2:17-18;**

> **"Then Daniel went to his house and made the decision known to Haniah, Mishael and Azariah his companions, that they might seek mercies from the God of heaven concerning this secret, so that Daniel and his companions might not perish with the rest of the wise men of Babylon."**

Later Daniel acknowledged the power of God and his ability to reveal secrets to his servants. In **Daniel 2:28,** he declared,

> **"But there is a God in heaven who reveals secrets …"**

Job wrote of God,

> **"He uncovers deep things out of darkness and brings the shadow of death to light" (Job 12:22).**

The Psalmist said in **Psalm 25:14,**
> **"The secret of the Lord is with those who fear Him, and He will show them His covenant."**

When the apostles were confronted with the choice of a replacement for Judas, they prayed a simple prayer, **"You, O Lord, who knows the hearts of all, show which of these two you have chosen" (Acts 1:24)** and God answered them.

Amos, the great prophet wrote,

> **"Surely the Lord God does nothing, unless he reveals his secret to his servants the prophets" (Amos 3:7).**

Paul told us,

> **"But God has revealed them to us, through His spirit. For the spirit searches all things, yes the deep things of God" (1 Corinthians 2:10).**

Solomon tells us,

> "The spirit of man is the candle of God
> searching all the inward parts of the belly"
> (Proverbs 20:27 KJV).

We need to be instructed. The Psalmist tells us that
God will instruct us and teach us in the way we should
go and guide us with His eye **(Psalms 32:8)**. Solomon
admonished his son,

> "Take firm hold of instruction, do not let go;
> keep her, for she is your life" (Proverbs 4:13).

He said in **Proverbs 15:32, "He who disdains
instruction despises his own soul..."** He further
advised in **Proverbs 23:12, 23**,

> "Apply your heart to instruction and your ears to
> words of knowledge... Buy the truth and do not
> sell it, also wisdom and instruction and
> understanding."

Being instructed is the cutting edge that the child of

God has. It is like having privileged information. Little wonder Solomon emphasized the importance of listening to instruction by his son. The instructed man rarely goes wrong because instruction is the light by which he avoids the pitfalls of life. Haste prevents us from listening to instruction. The instructed man will not be impulsive even when under pressure. He acts timely and accurately. Isaiah talked about how he was instructed,

> **"For the Lord spoke thus to me with a strong hand, and instructed me that I should not walk in the way of this people" (Isaiah 8:11).**

Instruction, wisdom, knowledge, guidance; these are your divine breakthrough. They are those things that distinguish you.

> **"For as many are led by the spirit of God, they are the sons of God" (Romans 8:14).**

EPILOGUE -
I AM INSTRUCTED

Have you ever paused before a great task or decision to ask for wisdom? The Bible says, **"Wisdom is the principal thing..."** **(Proverbs 4:7).** In the multitude of counselors, there is safety. The spirit has been promised to guide, direct and show us the way.

Are you an impulsive person? Stop to consider your actions and the consequences, before you leap. Are you always making choices? Stop now to ask God for the ability to choose right. God has promised to instruct us. Are you willing to wait to get the wisdom required from above? List your decisions and wait for instruction.

....

....

....

....

....

....

....

Say loud today and everyday before any task: 'Lord, thank you that I can hear a voice behind me. Thank you for ordering my path and steps. Thank you for showing me the way forward.'

AFFIRMATION - SIX

I PRESS FORWARD

"I PRESS toward the mark for the prize of the high calling of God in Christ Jesus" (Philippians 3:14 KJV).

This is an affirmation of persistence. When you have written your goals, and you know what God wants you to do, then press forward. You must not give room for discouragement. Paul said,

> **"I press toward the mark for the prize of the high calling of God in Christ Jesus" (Philippians 3:14).**

He also said,

> **"But none of these things move me" (Acts 20:24).**

I press toward the mark is your determination to be persistent in spite of the difficult situations. Someone once said, 'The secret to success is to start from the scratch and keep scratching.' R. C. Forbes said, 'If you can consistently do your best, the worst won't happen'? Abraham Lincoln, the great American President said, 'I am a slow walker but I never walk back.'

Failure has been described as the path of least persistence. A great writer once commented, 'Nothing in this world can take the place of persistence. Talent will not; nothing is more common than unsuccessful men with talent. Genius will not; unrewarded genius is almost a proverb. Education will not; the world is full of educated derelicts. Persistence and determination alone are omnipotent. The slogan 'Press on' has solved and always will solve the problems of the human race.'

When you have set your goal, then keep pressing on. Persistence is maintaining a finisher attitude. It means burning all the bridges behind you and holding on to your goal until you get there. Helen Keller, a woman who was rendered deaf, dumb and blind after a fever as a baby and who overcame all these physical challenges wrote: 'We can do anything we want as long as we stick to it long.' Jesus taught us the power of persistence. He said;

> **"...No man having put his hand on the plow and looking back is fit for the kingdom of God"** **(Luke 9:62).**

You must never look back. Thomas Edison was one of the greatest American inventors. Did you know he had less than three months of formal schooling? By his own estimation, he conducted ten thousand experiments that failed. Nevertheless, he pursued his goals and invented the electric light bulb, among many others. Today, he is one of the greatest men that ever lived. By passing through a road twice, you get accustomed to the journey. Think of Gideon and his army. The Bible says,

> **"And Gideon came to Jordan and passed over, he and the three hundred men that were with him,**

faint, yet pursuing them" (Judges 8:4 KJV).

The best way to look at **'I press'** is to imagine a woman about to put to bed. The midwives will say 'push.' Pushing is not easy. Anything that must be begotten from your being has to be pushed.

To achieve the seemingly impossible, we must persist. Can you beat the persistence of Abraham Lincoln, the former president of United States of America? He failed in business at age 22, ran for legislature at 23, again failed in business at 24, elected to legislature at 25, sweetheart died at 26, had a nervous breakdown at 27, defeated for speaker at 29, defeated for elector at 31, defeated for congress at 34, elected for congress at 37, defeated for congress at 39, defeated for senate at 46, defeated for vice president at 47, defeated for senate at 49 and finally elected president of United States of America at 51. He eventually achieved his goal because he never gave up.

The Hebrew writer said,

"Therefore we also, since we are surrounded by
so great a cloud of witnesses, let us lay aside
every weight and the sin which so easily
ensnares us, and let us run with endurance the
race that is set before us" (Hebrews 12:1).

He went further to instruct the Hebrew church,

"That ye be not slothful, but followers of them
who through faith and patience inherit the
promises" (Hebrews 6:12 KJV).

Emerson said, "That which we persist in doing
becomes easier, not that the nature of the task has
changed but our ability to do it has increased." Paul
wrote to the Corinthian church,

"Therefore my beloved brethren, be steadfast,
immoveable, always abounding in the work of
the Lord, knowing that your labour is not in vain
in the Lord" (1 Corinthians 16:58).

Don't forget, when you experience a resistance, it is
telling you to re-fire. When it seems you have failed, it
is not a call to retreat, but a challenge to put in extra
effort. Failure is not final; it is a process that will

invariably lead you to success if you can only persist.

Your will might propel you forward but persistence will get you there. The crown is only reserved for those who persist to the end. The importunate person will get to his goal. Even in prayers Jesus teaches us to be persistent until we see our desires accomplished.

> **"One day Jesus told his disciples a story to illustrate their need for constant prayer and to show them that they must never give up" (Luke 18:1 NLT).**

Oppositions are bound to stand in the way whenever we seek to accomplish something worthwhile. It simply confirms how precious what we are aiming to achieve. The most important thing is to develop a **'Relentless Forward Motion' (RFM).** Even if you must fall, fall forward and do not stay down but get up and keep going. No matter how many times you are knocked down, make sure you are not knocked out. Whether you are discouraged, acknowledged or not, celebrated or ignored, wounded or abandoned just keep moving forward. One day the whole world will stand in attention for you and the very people who had opposed you will commend you for your persistence. Press forward!

EPILOGUE - I PRESS FORWARD

Think of all the situations that have caused you to think of going back or withdrawing; friends, foes, failures and frustration of all kinds. Think of the joy, the glory and the trophies you will win, if you persist. Write down the advantages of persistence and the disadvantages if you quit.

....
....
....
....
....
....
....

Do you want to go into history as a quitter or a loser? Determine to press on regardless of the opposition, obstacles and occurrences of your life. Say loud: 'I am not a quitter, I press on.'

AFFIRMATION - SEVEN

I AM NOT WORTHY BUT MADE WORTHY

> "I am not worthy of the least of all the mercies and of all the truth which you have shown your servant..." (Genesis 32:10 NKJV).

If you are going to succeed, you must recognize the power of divine mercy. We are not metaphysicians; we are not just positive thinkers. The Christian's affirmation has its foundation in God. The best illustration of this affirmation is found in Jacob. He said in **Genesis 32:10-12,**

> "I am not worthy of the least of all the mercies and of all truth which thou hast showed unto thy servant; for with my staff I passed over this Jordan; and now I am become two bands. Deliver me, I pray thee, from the hand of Esau; for I fear him, lest he will come and smite me, and the mother with the children. And thou said, I will surely do thee good, and make thy seed as the

sand of the sea, which cannot be numbered for multitude." (KJV)

Paul said,

> "Therefore, we also pray always for you that our God would count you worthy of this calling and fulfill all the good pleasure of his goodness, and the work of faith with power" (2 Thessalonians 1:11)

'I am not worthy' indirectly declares that 'Lord, the glory goes back to you.' 'The honour goes back to you.' It is like a student who has thoroughly prepared for his examination and then kneels to pray, 'God, the horse is prepared for battle but the victory is of the Lord.'

> "So then, It is not of him who wills nor of him who runs but of God who shows mercy" (Romans 9:16).

Paul said in **2 Corinthians 3:5**

> "Not that we are sufficient of ourselves to think

**of anything as being from ourselves but our
sufficiency is from God."**

Not that when I say the word 'I can', I am already
sufficient but I look up to God for my sufficiency.
When faced with great infirmities, Paul pleaded with
God to remove it from him but God said,

**"...My grace is sufficient for you, for my strength
is made perfect in your weakness..." (2
Corinthians 12:8, 9)**

Grace is tapping God's power. It is releasing His
potential and ability into our lives. This is the secret
behind the life of the Lord Jesus Christ. When we
declare 'I am not worthy,' we are simply saying I am
the pipe God is the pump. I am the clay He is the
potter. It is not the language of the weakling; rather it
is acknowledging our humanity and affirming His
divinity; our fallibility and His infallibility. Any man
that will be great must first be little in his own eyes; to
that man God will reach out His hands.

With this affirmation, you become a channel God can

use to demonstrate His power and show forth His greatness to mankind. In **John 5:19,** Christ said,

> **"Most assuredly, I say unto you. The son can do nothing of himself, but what he sees the father do, for whatsoever he does the son also does in like manner."**

This is further affirmed in verse 30.

> **"I can of myself do nothing: as I hear, I judge and my judgement is just righteous, because I do not seek my own will but the will of the father who sent me."**

This affirmation liberates us from pride. Like James we begin to say,

> **"If the Lord wills, we shall live and do this or that"** **(James 4:15).**

Like Mary you can say,

> **"Behold the handmaid of the Lord, be it unto me according to thy word" (Luke 1:38).**

We can also say like Jehoshaphat of old, when confronted with the children of Ammon who came against him and the people of Isreal in battle,

> **"O our God, will you not judge them? For we have no power against this great multitude that is coming against us, nor do we know what to do but our eyes are upon you" (2 Chronicles 20:12).**

The Psalmist declared,

> **"Except the Lord builds the house, they labour in vain that build it. Except the Lord keeps the city, the watchman waketh but in vain" (Psalms 127:1).**

When you make this declaration, 'I am not worthy but made worthy,' you are telling the Lord to build your life, house and destiny. You are saying to him, 'be my shield and buckler.' As Jeremiah prayed long ago,

> **"O Lord, I know the way of man is not in himself: it is not in man who walks to direct his own steps" (Jeremiah 10:23).**

God is able to take us to our place in destiny. He is sufficient for us and through Him we can achieve our goals.

EPILOGUE - I AM NOT WORTHY BUT MADE WORTHY

Have you ever acknowledged your insufficiency or do you think you can do it on your own? Have you relegated God to the background in your search for fame? God can take you to where you are going if you will let Him. Think of all the areas of your life that you have not surrendered to God. Acknowledge the divine ability of God to bring your dreams to reality. Make a list of those areas you want God to control from now on.

....

....

....

....

Pray that God will help you to hand over the course of your life to Him in faith.

A CALL TO CHRIST

This book is not just about positive affirmation or 'mind over matter.' The whole essence is to bring you to a relationship with the living God who through His love sent his Son, Jesus Christ, to die for us.

Your affirmation will only be productive if you have constant fellowship with the master. Jesus said,

> **"All that the Father gives me will come to me, and the one who comes to me I will by no means cast out"** (John 6:37).

Paul wrote:

> **"Therefore, if anyone is in Christ, he is a new**

creation; old things have passed away; behold, all things have become new" (1 Corinthians 5:17).

Jesus emphasized the need to put new wine into new bottles. Mere affirmation without a change of heart is 'philosophizing' which makes you mentally rich and spiritually poor. Regardless of your past, you can begin today and have a great tomorrow. Why not give Jesus a place in your life and make Jesus your Lord and Master. I assure you it will be the beginning of great things in your life. You can join in this simple prayer:

"O Lord, I receive your unconditional love today. I acknowledge that I am a sinner in need of your mercy and forgiveness. I confess my sins before you. I renounce the devil and the world and I wholeheartedly commit my life to you. Come and live inside me and be my Lord and Saviour. Establish your lordship in my heart and grant me the grace to continually live in oneness with you in Jesus name, Amen."

As you begin to declare the affirmations in this book, your life will experience a great transformation. For further information, help or if you want to share your experience with me,

Please write:

Rev. Prof. G. E. Erhabor
P. O. Box 1154, Ile-Ife
gregerhabor7@yahoo.com
www.spokesmancom.org

www.ingramcontent.com/pod-product-compliance
Lightning Source LLC
Chambersburg PA
CBHW070555030426
42337CB00016B/2504